A Cat, a Kid, a Dog

Written by Charlotte Raby

Illustrated by Camilla Galindo

Collins

a dog

a kid
· · · ·

a dog

a kid

a cat
. . . .

dig

a cat

dig

a sock

a cap

a sock

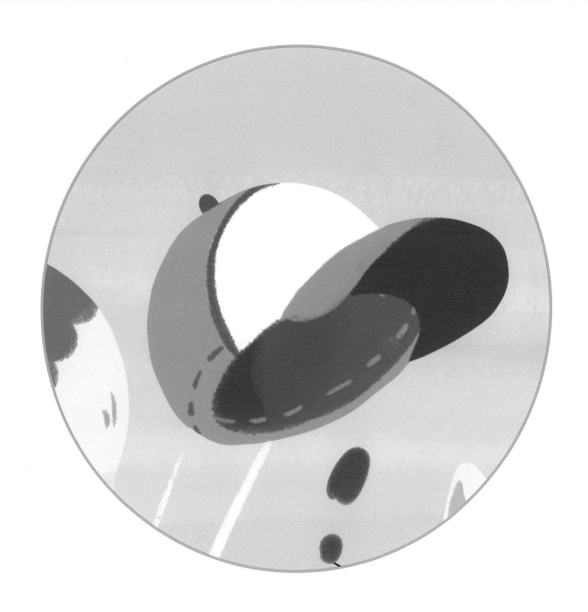

a cap

/c/

14

🐾 Review: After reading 🐾

Use your assessment from hearing the children read to choose any GPCs and words that need additional practice.

Read 1: Decoding

- Read pages 3, 6 and 10. After each page, ask: Can you point to the letter or letters that make the /c/ sound? (*k, c, ck*)
- Look at the "I spy sounds" pages (14–15) together. Ask the children to point out as many things that they can in the picture that begin with the /c/ sound. (*cow, crow, cabbages, carrots, caterpillar, cricket, cap, cat*)

Read 2: Vocabulary

- Go back over the three spreads and discuss the pictures. Encourage children to talk about details that stand out for them. Use a dialogic talk model to expand on their ideas and recast them in full sentences as naturally as possible.
- Work together to expand vocabulary by naming objects in the pictures that children do not know.
- Reread pages 6 and 7. Ask: What does the dog do? (*digs*)

Read 3: Comprehension

- Discuss the picture on pages 14 and 15. Ask the children:
  - What can you see on the farm?
  - Which things did the dog find? (*cap, sock*)
  - Who are the three main animals in the book? (*cat, kid, dog*)
  - What other animals do you know? (e.g. *chickens, chick, cow*)